# SWEARING CATS

THIS COLORING BOOK BELONGS

# Dear colorist,

Thank you for choosing our Swearing Cats Coloring Book! We hope it brings you creative, relaxing hours filled with joy and a sense of tranquility.

Ilf you have a moment, we would greatly appreciate it if you could leave a review on Amazon. Your feedback not only helps us in shaping our coloring books but also assists others in finding their perfect book. Thank you for your support. Happy mindful coloring!

Warm regards,
The **YOUR**notes Team

Leave some feedback & follow us on Amazon.com

*The shown QR Codes will lead you to your last orders page on www.amazon.com

**YOUR NOTES**
MADE WITH LOVE

# Every cat is sooo unique ...

We try always to give a little extra spice with our coloring books. To give you the chance to build an unforgettable memory we decided to make this book interactive. Write us a mail (YOURnotes.Publishing@gmail.com) till end of December 2024 with your cats special characteristics and **we try to create a themed coloring page for you.**

# Paperselection

We opt for standard-quality paper to keep things affordable, given the limited paper options available on Amazon. To avoid ink or marker bleeding, you can place a thicker sheet behind the page you're coloring. We appreciate your understanding of our paper choice

A blank sheet of paper prevents bleeding

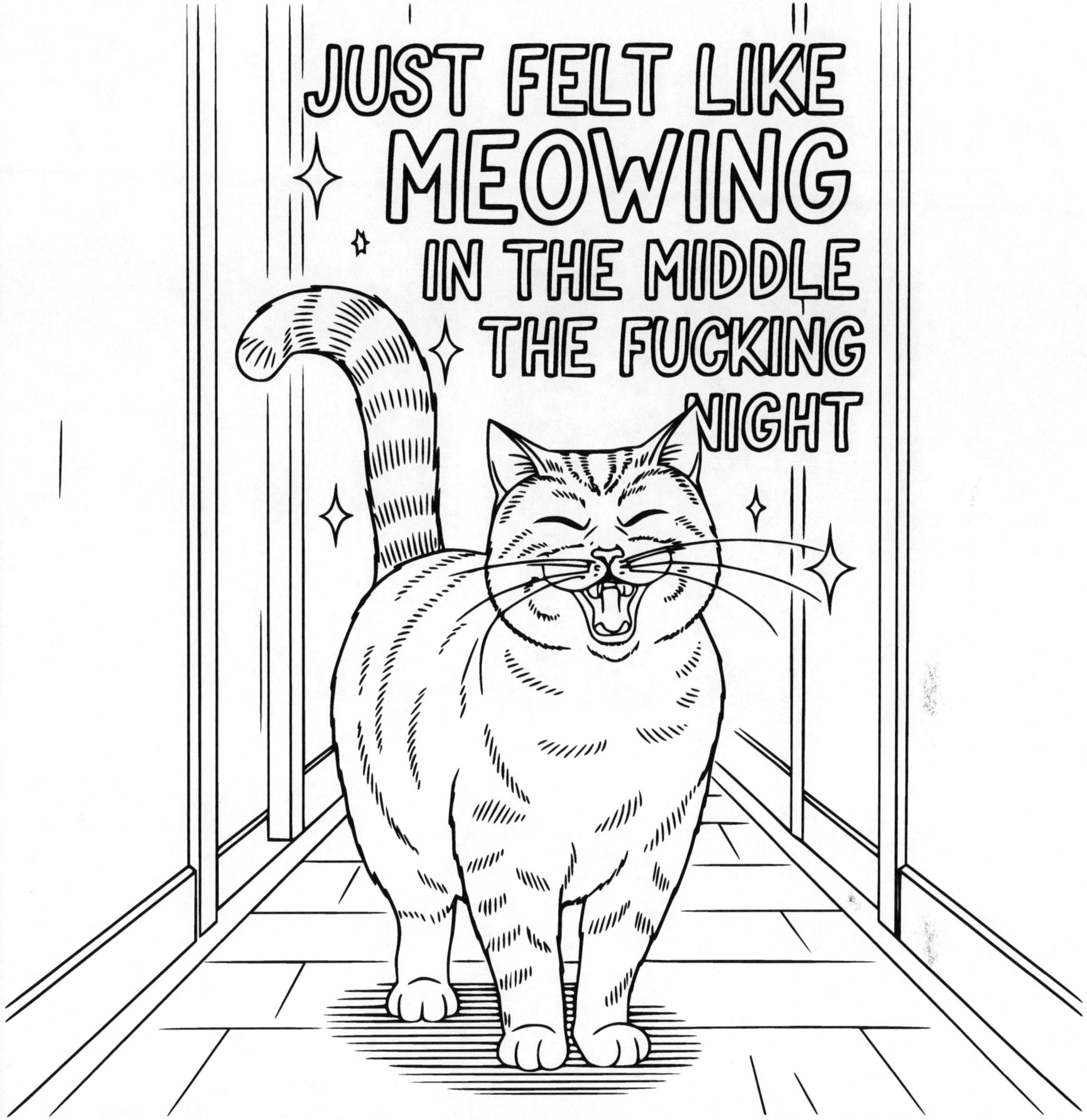
JUST FELT LIKE
MEOWING
IN THE MIDDLE
THE FUCKING
NIGHT

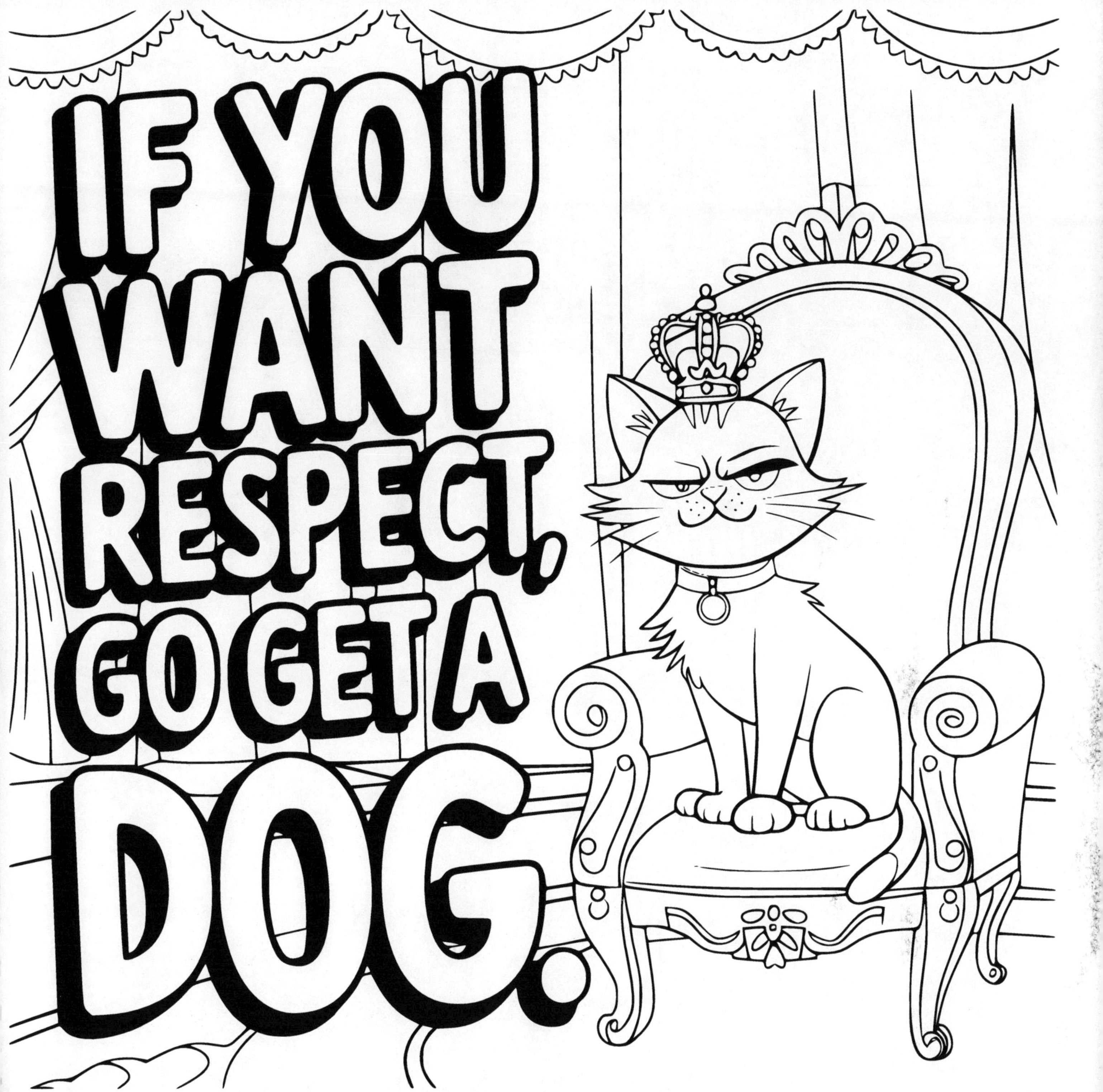
IF YOU
WANT
RESPECT,
GO GET A
DOG.

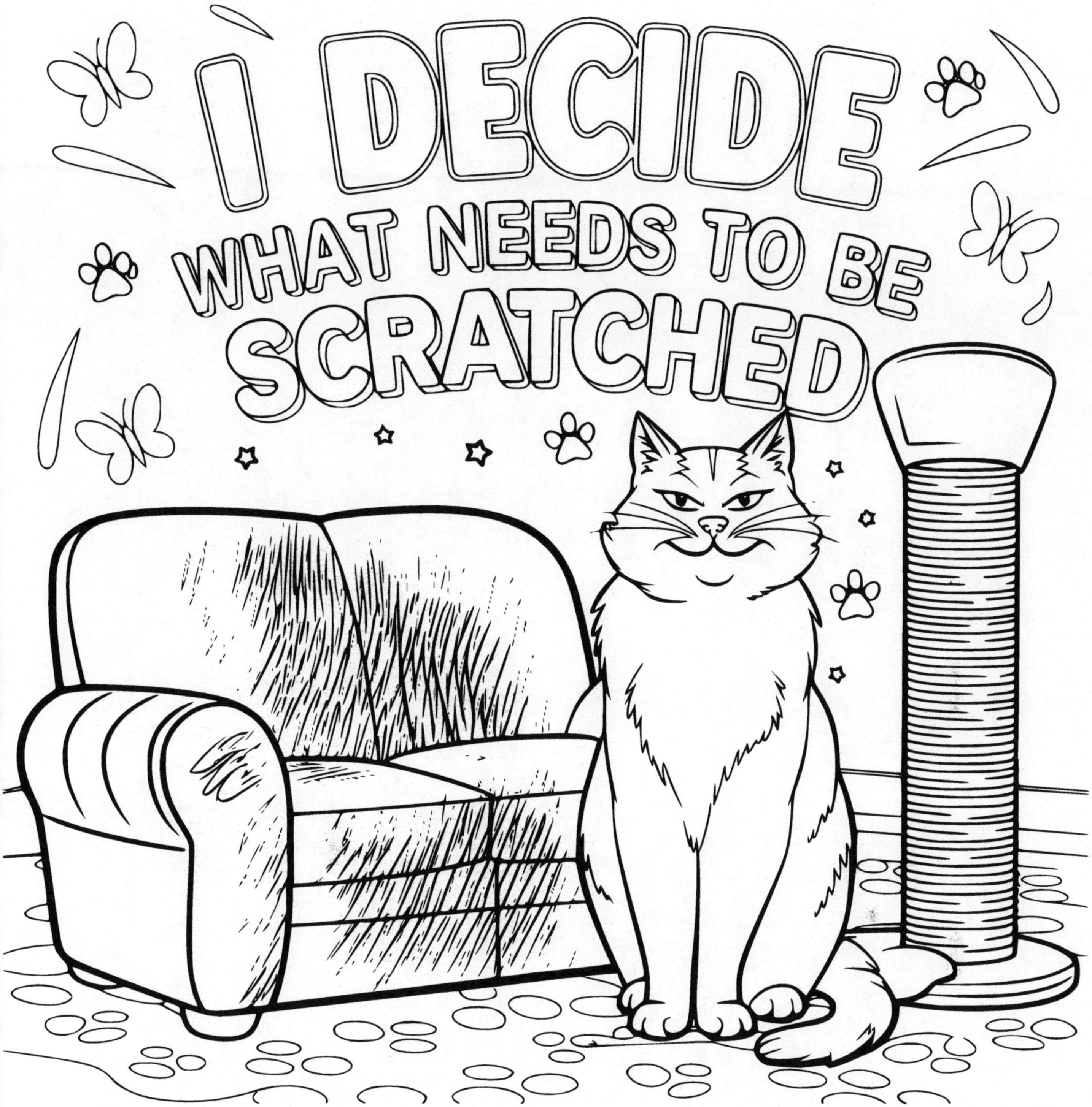
I DECIDE
WHAT NEEDS TO BE
SCRATCHED

JUST A CAT
ON A
MISSION:
HUNTING
SHADOWS
AND YOUR
BULLSHIT!

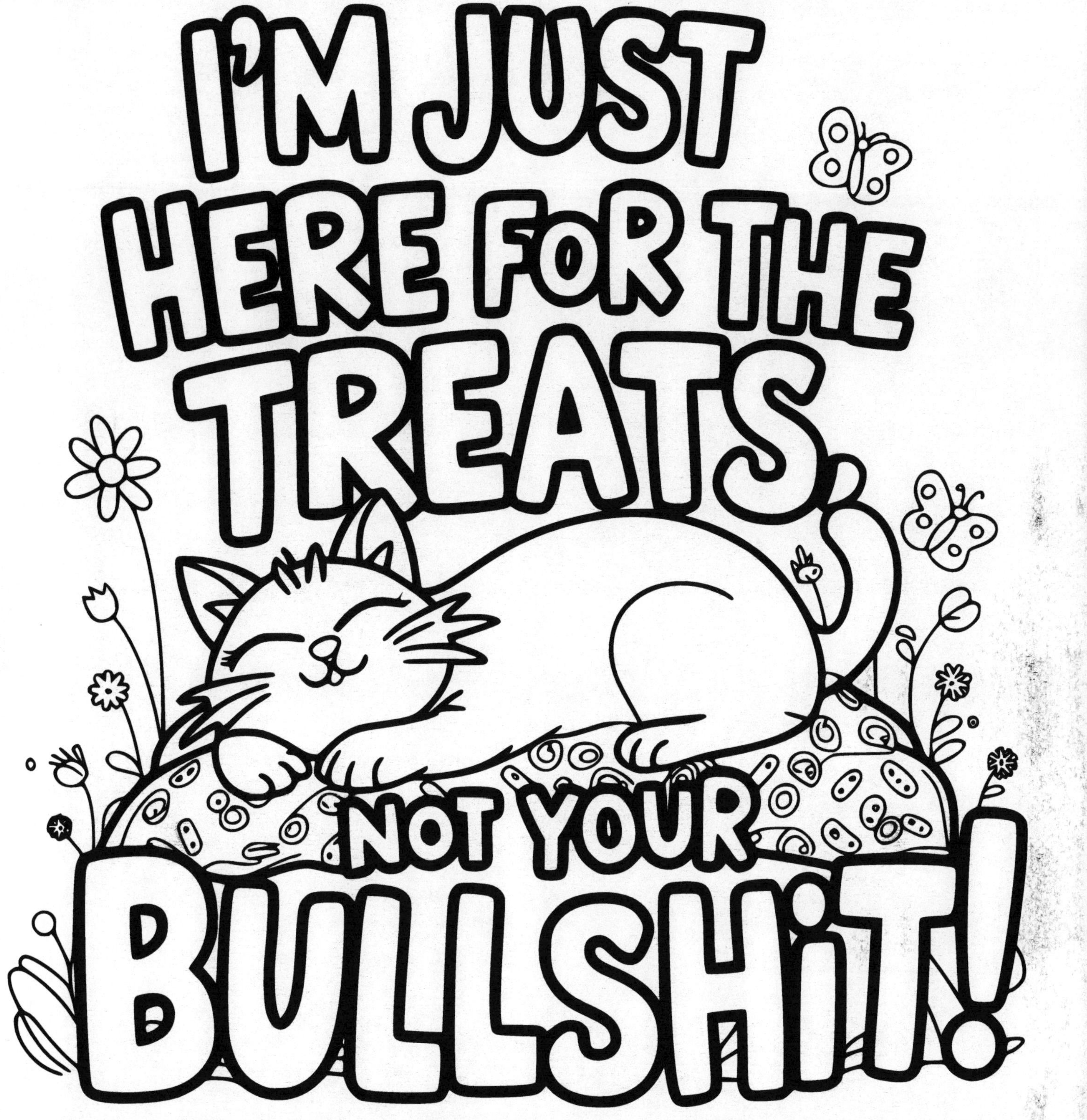
I'M JUST
HERE FOR THE
TREATS,
NOT YOUR
BULLSHIT!

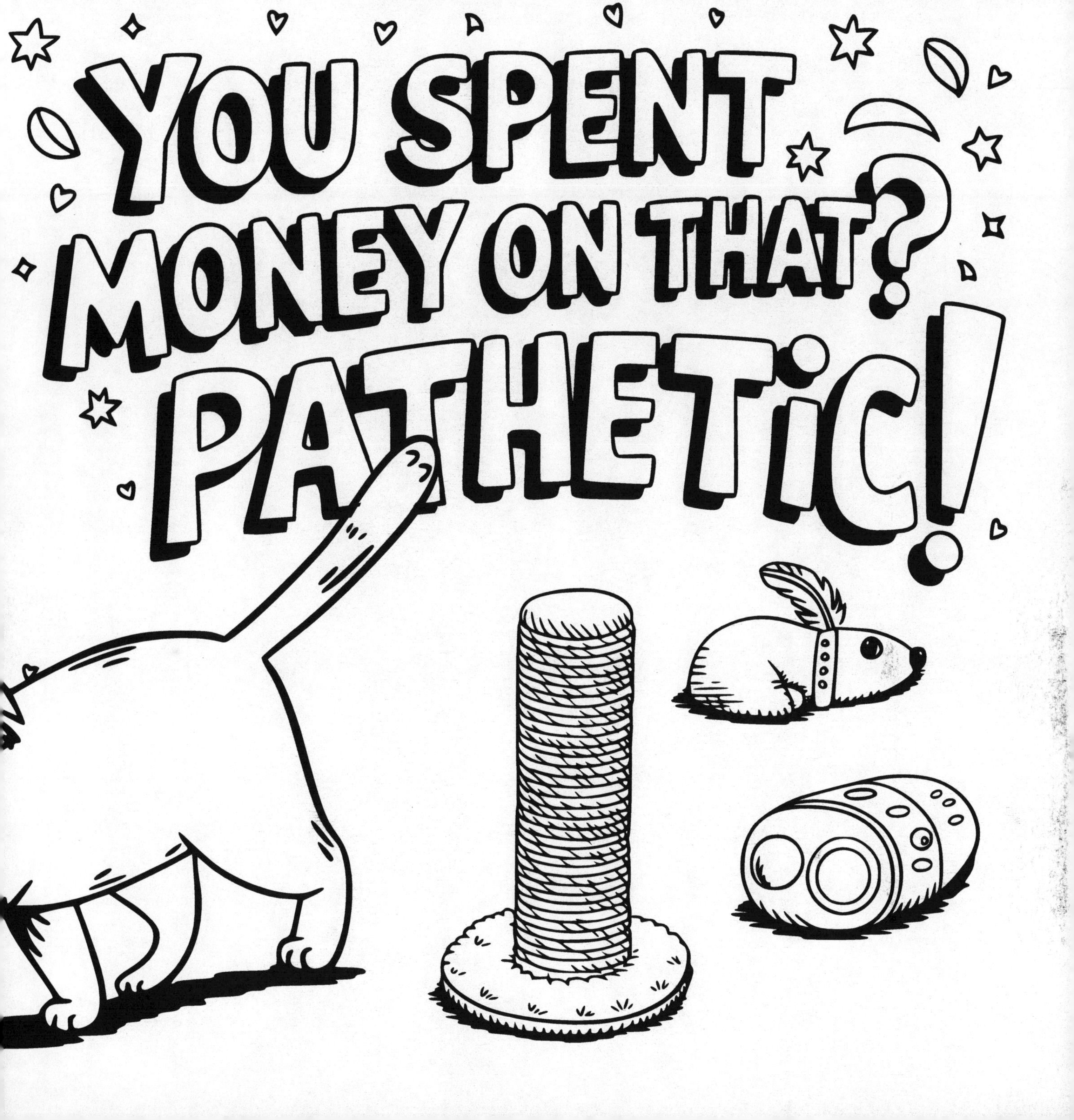
YOU SPENT MONEY ON THAT?
PATHETIC!

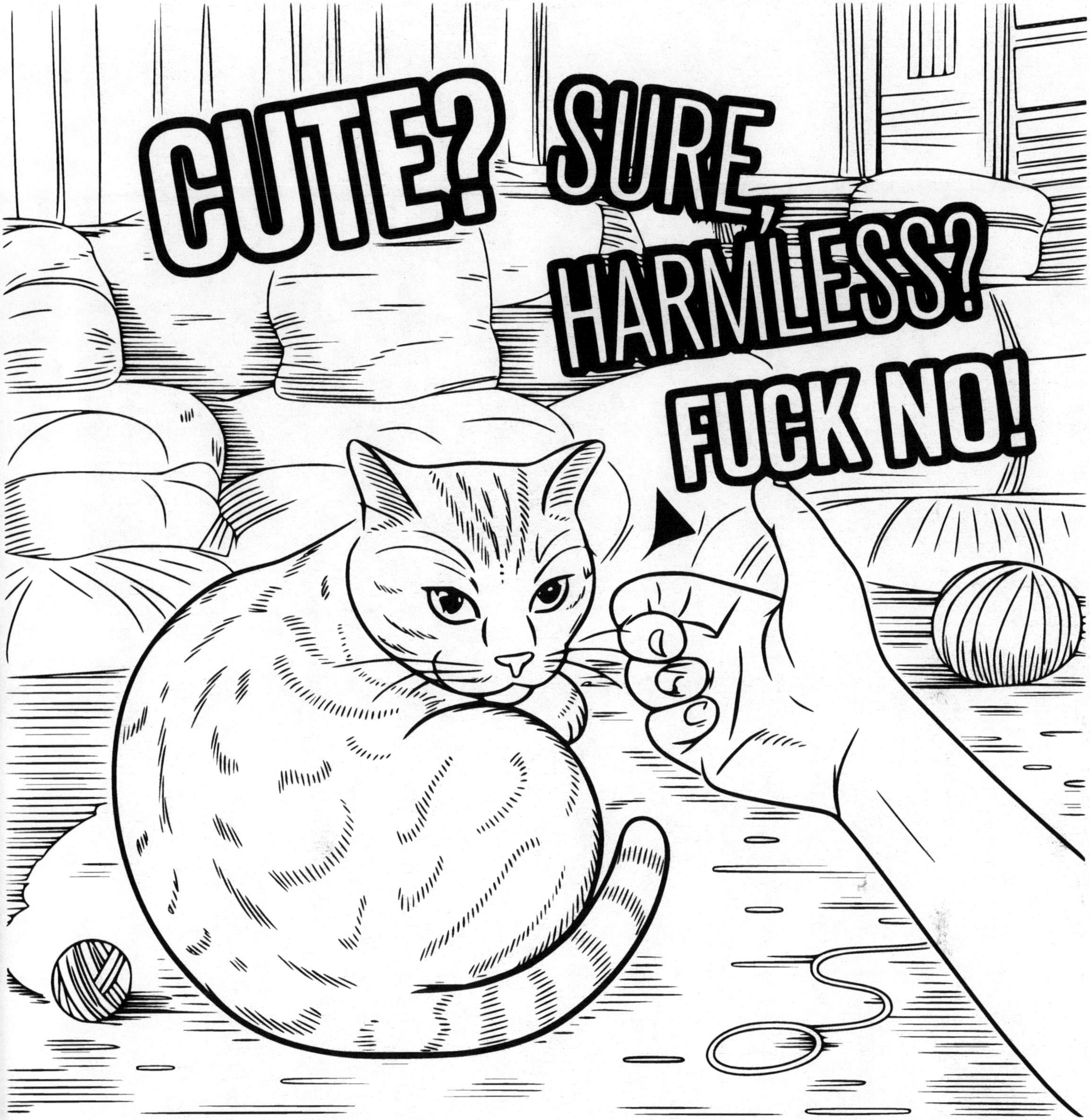
CUTE? SURE,
HARMLESS?
FUCK NO!

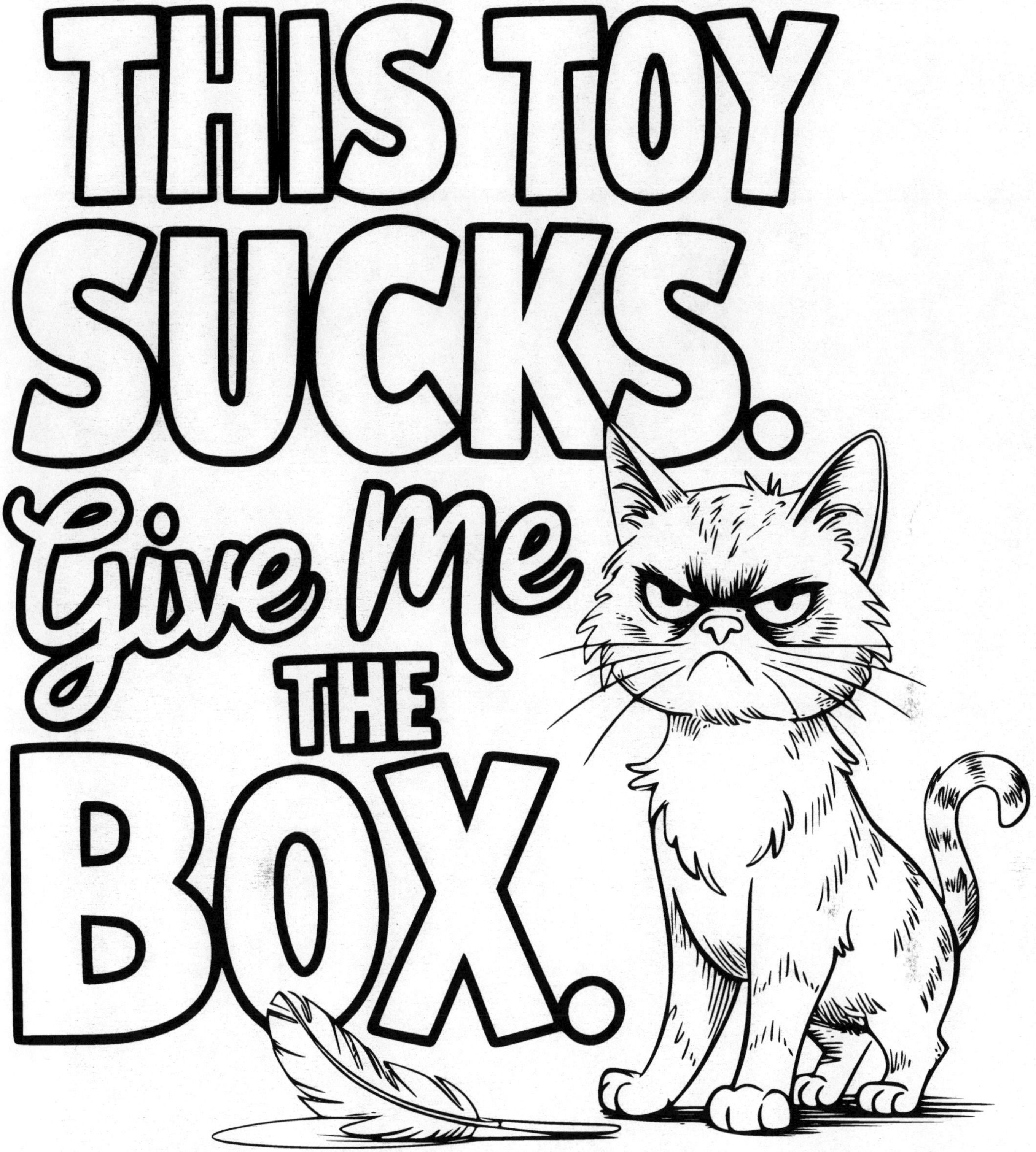
THIS TOY
SUCKS.
Give Me
THE
BOX.

I'll let you pet me...

UNTIL I

FUCKING

WON'T

# Self-care isn't Selfish

# IT'S FUCKING NECESSARY!

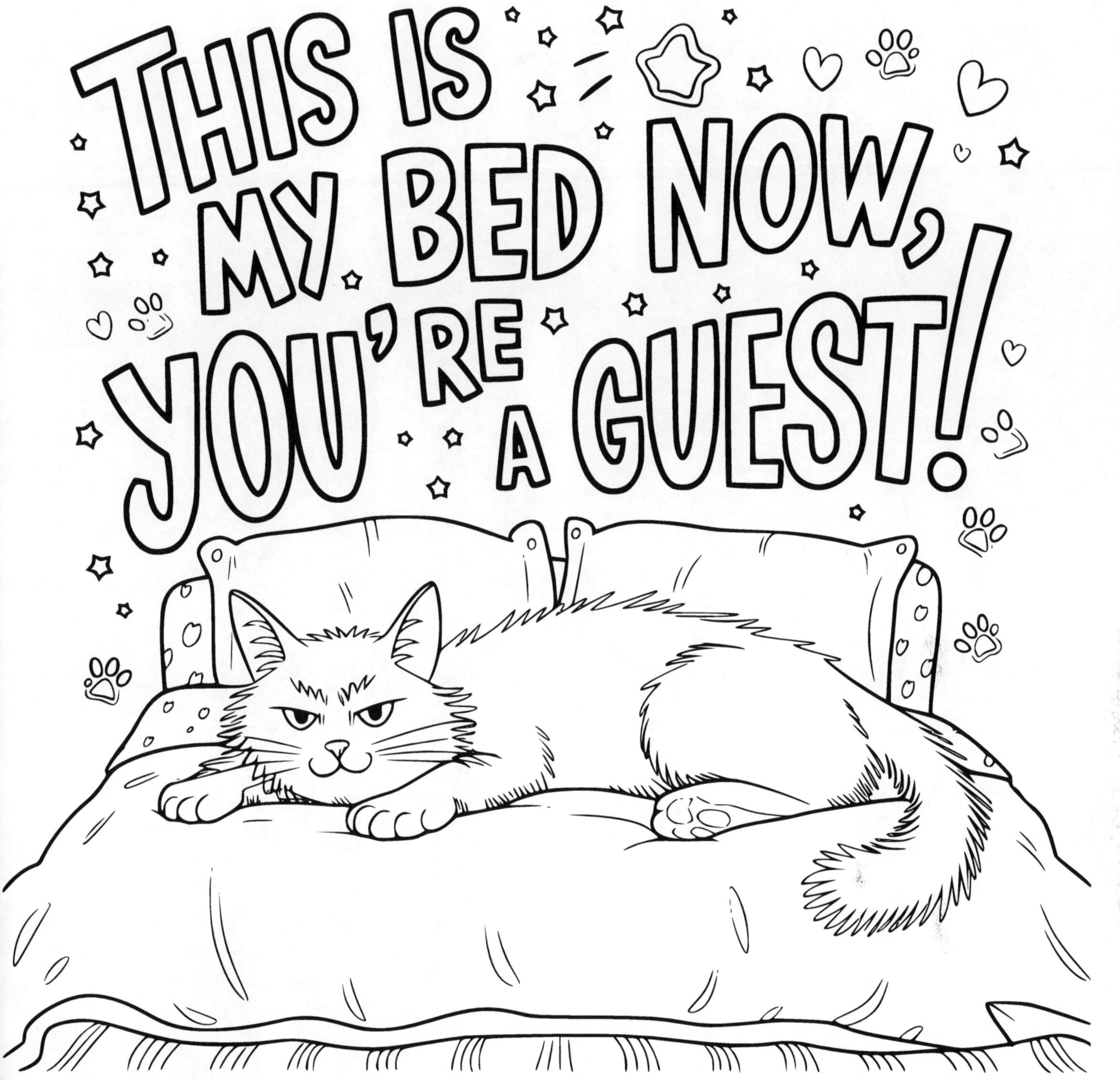
THIS IS MY BED NOW, YOU'RE A GUEST!

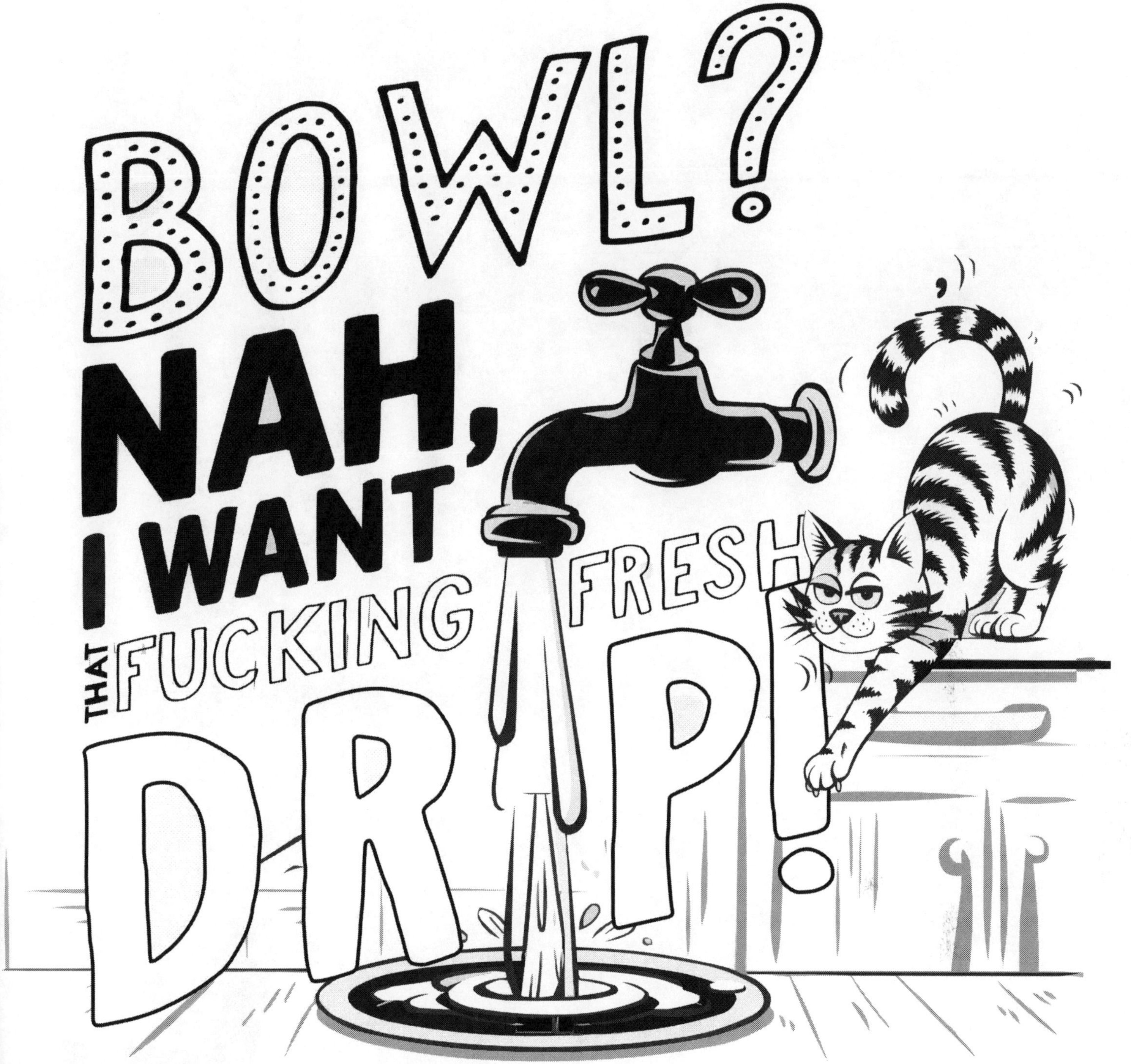
BOWL?
NAH,
I WANT
THAT FUCKING FRESH
DRIP!

YOUR WORDS ARE JUST BACKGROUND NOISE TO MY Fabulous LiFE!

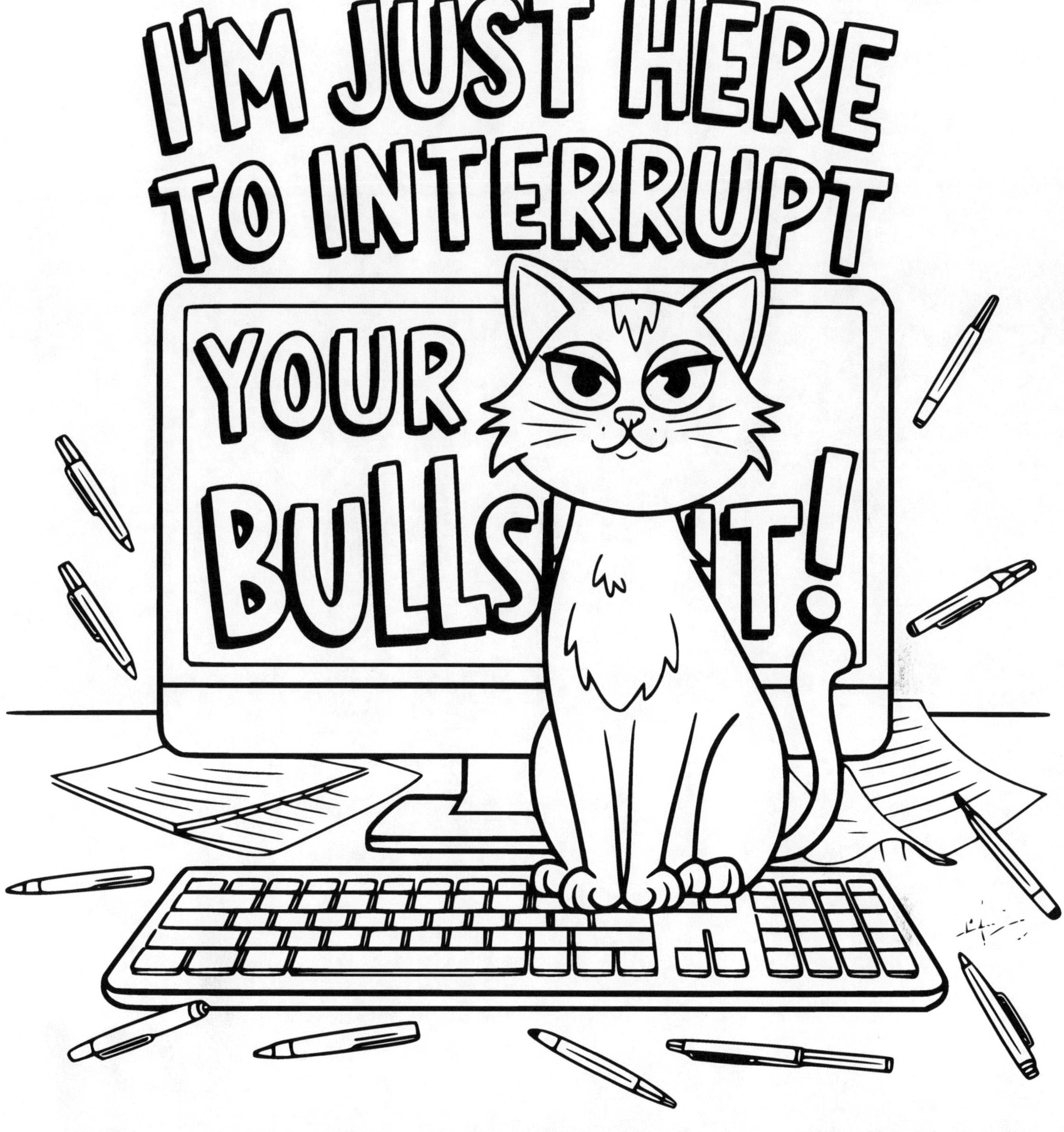
I'M JUST HERE
TO INTERRUPT
YOUR
BULLS
T!

# DID YOU
## *enjoy the book ?*

Share your experience with others &
feel free to rate us on Amazon.com

★ ★ ★ ★ ★

We are very grateful for any
feedback.

Leave some feedback &
follow us on Amazon.com

YOUR**NOTES**
MADE WITH LOVE

*The shown QR Codes will lead
you to your last orders page on
www.amazon.com*

©YOURnotes Publishing – Wiesbadener Str. 5 – 01159 Dresden / Germany – YOURnotes.Publishing@gmail.com
Inner graphics designed by: freepik.com – Cover graphics: freepik.com –
Author / Composition of elements: Thomas Eckstein

# DO YOU NEED SOMETHING FOR
## *your mindfulness ?*

### Mindfulness Coloring Book For Adults (Volume 1)

ISBN: 979-8499178775
50 Animal motifs and floral patterns in mandala style on 100 pages

| | |
|---|---|
| Format: | 8.5 x 8.5in |
| Complexity: | ★★★★★ |
| Animal motifs: | ★★★★☆ |
| Floral patterns: | ★☆☆☆☆ |

www.amazon.com/dp/
B09JV97Y6P

### Mindfulness Coloring Book For Adults (Volume 2)

ISBN: 979-8474606057
50 Animal motifs and floral patterns in mandala style on 100 pages

| | |
|---|---|
| Format: | 8.5 x 8.5in |
| Complexity: | ★★★★☆ |
| Animal motifs: | ★★★★☆ |
| Floral patterns: | ★☆☆☆☆ |

www.amazon.com/dp/
B09F558C2L

Made in United States
Troutdale, OR
11/25/2024

25213611R00063